STRONG, HEALTHY GIRLS

USING SOCIAL MEDIA RESPONSIBLY

By Emma Huddleston

CONTENT CONSULTANT

Dr. Amy Bellmore
Professor of Human Development
University of Wisconsin–Madison

Essential Library
An Imprint of Abdo Publishing | abdobooks.com

abdobooks.com

Published by Abdo Publishing, a division of ABDO, PO Box 398166, Minneapolis, Minnesota 55439.

Printed in the United States of America, North Mankato, Minnesota.
082020
012021

Cover Photo: Shutterstock Images
Interior Photos: Shutterstock Images, 8, 11, 23, 32, 34, 38, 41, 73, 76, 90, 93; Rocketclips, Inc./Shutterstock Images, 13; iStockphoto, 17, 44, 50; Lupe Rodriguez/Shutterstock Images, 20; Panida Wijitpanya/iStockphoto, 25; Andrey Popov/Shutterstock Images, 28–29; Robert Daly/iStockphoto, 47; Gail Johnson/Shutterstock Images, 48; Lilawa.com/Shutterstock Images, 56; Wave Break Media/Shutterstock Images, 59; DGL Images/iStockphoto, 65; Omg Images/iStockphoto, 68; Zoriana Zaitseva/Shutterstock Images, 70–71; Courtney Hale/iStockphoto, 75; Mstudio Images/iStockphoto, 80; Vera Petrunina/Shutterstock Images, 83; Mansong Suttakarn/Shutterstock Images, 85; Krakenimages.com/Shutterstock Images, 86; Alena Ozerova/Shutterstock Images, 96; Syda Productions/Shutterstock Images, 99

Editor: Megan Ellis
Series Designer: Nikki Nordby

Library of Congress Control Number: 2019954324
Publisher's Cataloging-in-Publication Data

Names: Huddleston, Emma, author.
Title: Using social media responsibly / by Emma Huddleston
Description: Minneapolis, Minnesota : Abdo Publishing, 2021 | Series: Strong, healthy girls | Includes online resources and index.
Identifiers: ISBN 9781532192241 (lib. bdg.) | ISBN 9781098210144 (ebook)
Subjects: LCSH: Mass media and girls--Juvenile literature. | Internet--Safety measures--Juvenile literature. | Teenage girls in popular culture--Juvenile literature. | Body image in girls--Juvenile literature. | Cyberbullying--Juvenile literature. | On-line etiquette--Juvenile literature.
Classification: DDC 155.533--dc23

CONTENTS

DR. AMY

Amy Bellmore is fascinated by humans and inspired by teens. She works as a professor of human development in the Department of Educational Psychology at the University of Wisconsin–Madison, where she conducts research on the peer relationships of adolescents and teaches courses on adolescent development. She earned a PhD in developmental psychology at the University of Connecticut. While she did not declare a major in psychology until the middle of her sophomore year in college, she has evidence that she was destined to study teens from a work aptitude test she took her sophomore year in high school. Based on the results of the test about her interests and skills, she discovered that the best job for her was as a research psychologist. Now that she has worked in that career for almost 20 years, she is happy to verify that the test was correct.

During her career, Amy has conducted numerous studies on the social experiences of teens which have been published in more than 60 articles and book chapters. Most of these studies took place through partnerships with public middle and high schools across Wisconsin that share the goal of promoting the welfare of adolescents. Following the leads of the teens themselves, who have moved parts of their lives to online spaces, Amy's most recent research attends to the ways teens use social media to create and maintain their social relationships. Amy loves using social media herself and finds this research area particularly exciting because teens create and transform technology in such ways that she is always getting to learn something new.

Amy also serves as an associate editor for the Journal of Research on Adolescence, which is the flagship journal for the Society of Research on Adolescence, a community of researchers dedicated to the well-being of adolescents. In her non-work life, she stays on the pulse of youth culture (and generally enjoys rocking out) by regularly attending concerts of pop culture icons. Amy lives in Madison, Wisconsin, and Los Angeles, California, with her adolescent puggles, Presley and Riddock.

TAKE IT FROM ME

While social media can be a fun way to chat with friends or catch up on people's lives, it can also be downright exhausting. You might be unsure how much time is too much to spend on social media. Or you might be unsure how to protect yourself online from identity theft or cyberbullying. Seeing other people's perfect posts and seemingly perfect lives may make you sad or upset. In the world of social media, it's important to talk to your friends, family, and other trusted adults about how to make the right choices online.

During adolescence, many girls create social media profiles or increase the amount of time they spend online. Your best friend from elementary school may go to a different middle or high school. Or you may find people around the world who share the same interests as you when it seems like no one in your town likes the same music, TV show, or movies as you do. Unfortunately, lots of things that come with the excitement of social media can be emotional. People may interpret posts differently, and some people might take offense at these messages.

Part of what makes social media so tricky is that it is a major part of society. Girls can use social media in school, at home, and at any time of day. Many apps and websites let people connect by sharing photos, videos, and text. As you begin to develop into an adult, the choices you make about how you spend your time and who you interact with online can be challenging. In some situations, you will have to make tough decisions and answer difficult questions. Perhaps the most important questions you will face have to do with what you really want and what feels right to you. Being honest with yourself will help you find the right balance of social media in your life.

The key to it all is figuring out how to keep yourself informed and prepared to handle sticky situations, while still enjoying the fun and convenience of social media.

XOXO,
EMMA

CHAPTER ONE

MEETING NEW PEOPLE

Social media makes it easy to learn about different people and situations. You can see which pages or posts a person likes. You can read comments and captions to see whether you agree or disagree with someone's opinion. And you can send direct messages to someone if you want to talk more personally without everyone else seeing your conversation. Some people form friendships with people they meet through liking posts or blogging about the same content. They may use social media to interact with a more diverse group of people than is available in their neighborhoods or schools.

While scrolling through social media, you see plenty of familiar faces, but you also see strangers. Sometimes those strangers later become your friends. However, relationships that begin online come with certain risks. People can hide their true identity behind a screen. Trolls intentionally bully or upset others online because they can remain anonymous. Catfish create fake profiles and pretend to be different ages or genders than they really are. People who have bad intentions can take advantage of social media to target others.

It's important to be cautious when talking to strangers on the internet, especially if you plan to meet up with them in person. Use your social media smarts and trust your intuition. Tonya met a friend on Tumblr, but when the girls decided to meet up in person, she was still nervous. See how she handled meeting someone she knew from the internet for the first time in real life.

TONYA'S STORY

At first, Tonya used Tumblr only to reblog photography that she found interesting and wanted to re-create in her art class. Sometimes she'd look for funny memes or GIFs to send her friends too. But after a few months, Tonya started reblogging more and more posts about her favorite TV shows. Some people made memes about the characters. Other people wrote fan fiction about the characters who were in an on-again, off-again relationship. Some even made YouTube playlists full of songs and music videos that reminded them of the TV show.

One of Tonya's favorite things to scroll through was fan art. She loved seeing how different people drew the characters and what types of funny situations they got into. One of her favorite artists, Aniyah, liked to draw comics based on the TV show. For months, Tonya had liked all of Aniyah's posts, even the ones that were just sketches or works in progress. She commented on some of them too.

One day when Tonya logged on to Tumblr, she had a direct message from Aniyah. She clicked on the envelope in the corner of her screen. Aniyah had messaged, "Thanks for all the positive comments and likes! It gives me confidence to post more artwork when I get reactions like yours."

"Of course! You're really talented!" Tonya typed in a response. She was glad that she'd made Aniyah's day.

The next day, Tonya had another message from Aniyah in her inbox. "I'm trying to figure out what to draw based on last week's episode," Aniyah said.

"There were so many good scenes!" Tonya wrote back.

"What should I pick? Which one was your favorite?"

Tonya grinned. None of her friends at school watched the same show, so she'd been *dying* for someone to talk about the episode with. She sent Aniyah back a two-paragraph response. She was worried for a moment that it was too much, but when Aniyah sent back an equally long message, Tonya laughed. Aniyah seemed just as excited to talk about the show as she was.

TALK ABOUT IT

- **How do you feel about interacting with strangers online? What are some risks? What are some benefits?**
- **Have you ever met someone online? If yes, how did you get to know each other? If not, how would you start a conversation with someone new?**
- **Aniyah felt encouraged by Tonya's likes and comments. What are other ways social media can be a positive experience for people?**

Aniyah seemed just as excited to talk about the show as she was.

***

Tonya and Aniyah messaged and video chatted more and more over the next few weeks. They bonded over their favorite episodes and even decided to rewatch the first season at the same time. While watching and eating popcorn, Tonya and Aniyah messaged each other. Tonya was surprised to discover that Aniyah lived only an hour away. They'd even been to some of the same stores and other places in the area.

One day, Tonya and Aniyah decided they wanted to meet. They had been talking for months and felt like close friends.

Tonya had recently helped Aniyah find some articles for a tough history paper she had to write, and Aniyah supported Tonya while she panicked over how to ask out her crush in her Spanish class.

"You know, we should get lunch together sometime," Aniyah texted one Saturday afternoon while they were talking about what they wanted to happen on the show next season. "I'd love for us to talk offline!"

"That would be nice," Tonya agreed. They'd video chatted a few times, but that wasn't the same as gushing with a friend in the same space.

They'd video chatted a few times, but that wasn't the same as gushing with a friend in the same space.

The girls decided they would meet at the mall that was about halfway between their two houses. They could grab lunch in the food court. After deciding on a date and time, Tonya signed off Skype. She was a little nervous to meet someone she had met online for the first time, even though she felt like she knew Aniyah well. She decided to talk with her mom about her hesitations.

"Hey, Mom," Tonya said, walking into the kitchen. "Do you think it's OK for me to meet up with Aniyah in person?"

"That's the friend you met online who loves the same show as you, right?" her mom asked.

"Yeah," Tonya replied.

"Well, have you already made plans?"

"Yeah, we talked about meeting at the mall and getting lunch in the food court."

"That sounds like fun!" her mom said. She smiled. "Meeting in a public place and for a certain period of time is smart. That way other people will be around when you're hanging out and I'll know when to expect you back in case something goes wrong. But based on what you've told me about her, I think you and Aniyah will have a good time!"

Tonya felt her nerves disappear. "I think so too. Thanks, Mom," Tonya said.

***

On the day the girls were scheduled to meet, Tonya asked her mom to drive her to the mall. She also filled her mom in on details about Aniyah and their plan to meet.

TALK ABOUT IT

- **If you were going to meet up with someone you befriended online, what place would you feel most comfortable meeting? Is there an activity you could do together?**
- **Do you prefer meeting people online or in person? Explain your answer.**
- **What did Tonya do well when she thought about meeting up with Aniyah? In what ways did she practice good internet safety?**

"So this is what Aniyah looks like," Tonya said, showing Aniyah's profile to her mom after they parked in the mall parking lot.

"OK, and you said you're just getting some food, so it might only be an hour?" her mom asked.

"Yeah, and I'll have my phone with me the whole time if I need you."

"Great! I'll have mine too," her mom said. They walked inside together. Then, Tonya's mom left to do some shopping in a nearby store.

"Just let me know when you're done," she said. "And have fun!"

Tonya smiled and waved at her mom. She took a seat at one of the food court tables and waited for Aniyah to arrive. She was glad they had chosen to meet in the mall. Having lots of people around made Tonya feel safer.

A few minutes later, Aniyah walked in, and Tonya recognized her immediately. She waved, and Aniyah's face broke into a grin.

A few minutes later, Aniyah walked in, and Tonya recognized her immediately.

"Hi!" Aniyah said. "I'm so glad we finally get to meet!"

"Me too!" Tonya said. The girls ate their lunches and talked for an hour.

Tonya didn't realize how fast time was passing until she felt her phone buzzing in her pocket. Her mom was calling because it was time to go. Tonya and Aniyah eventually said goodbye, and Tonya was relieved their first in-person meeting had gone smoothly.

ASK THE EXPERT

Tonya was excited to meet a new friend who was also a fan of her favorite TV show, but nervous because she'd never seen Aniyah in real life before. Being careful about meeting someone in person for the first time helped Tonya feel safe and comfortable.

New devices and websites give people more ways to meet online. Overall, about one-third of people whose relationship started online end up meeting each other in person. The number of friendships, business relationships, romantic relationships, and other relationships have increased in recent decades alongside the rise of new technologies. Social networks play a part in close and distant friendships. In 2017, millions of people in the United States found romantic partners online.

While relationships with people who you'd never meet otherwise can be risky, they can also lead to many benefits. Friends can talk at any time of day or without being in the same room. People struggling with a certain illness or problem can find support from others who have been through it before. Girls can create valuable friendships online when they take time getting to know someone. You may find yourself creating close, meaningful friendships with someone online who lives across the world. Or, like Tonya, you may discover they live close by after all!

GET HEALTHY

- Be kind. You can meet wonderful people online if you take a chance to get to know them.
- Take it slow. Don't rush to share personal information with someone you just met online.
- Before meeting in person, try talking on the phone. Not only will you have a chance to talk but you can protect yourself. It is harder to fake a phone call than it is to fake photos.
- Meet in a public place. Being in a busy or open place can give you something to do together as well as make sure people are around to help if you need them.
- Alert family and friends. Make sure trusted people are aware that you are meeting someone for the first time. You could also plan to call, text, or ride with them to or from the meeting.

THE LAST WORD FROM EMMA

To me, meeting people online feels less stressful because there is no pressure to form a friendship. Just as easily as I started liking their posts, I can stop. It's important to remember that unfollowing someone doesn't necessarily mean you don't like that person. It just means you don't want to follow them on a social media account! That goes for people who follow you too. They may unfollow you for a variety of reasons, and that's OK.

Of course, when I really click with someone online, I want to meet them in person. We can safely schedule a time to meet and bring our friendship off-screen and into the real world. I've made some wonderful friends just by liking their photographs or the art they make!

CHAPTER TWO

STAYING CONNECTED

You probably have some form of social media, whether it's to share pictures, talk to friends, or keep up with what's going on in your town. Social media can be fun, and it makes staying connected simple. You can add a photo to your story, livestream a concert, and chat with others who might have similar interests or enjoy going to the same events.

You may also find it easier to keep in touch with people online than in person. The only place you have to travel is to a computer or smartphone, and suddenly you can video chat or message with a friend who lives across the country. If you have social anxiety or struggle to talk to people in person, staying connected using social media may feel easier and less stressful. For these reasons and many more, teens spend a lot of time together online every day. In fact, 60 percent of teens spent time with friends online daily in 2018. A study found that they texted and used social media most often when on a device such as a smartphone.

However, sometimes it can be good to take a step back from social media and the internet and reconnect with people offline. It's easy to get caught up in how often people post or the content they are sharing and not actually engage with the people themselves. Naomi found that out when she got annoyed with her friend Grace over social media.

NAOMI'S STORY

"No, no, do the filter with the dog ears," Sid told Naomi. Naomi swiped through the photo filters on Snapchat until she got to the right one. An image of dog ears appeared above each of their heads. *Click*. Naomi snapped the picture. She tapped the screen and wrote "Miss you" as the caption. Then she sent the snap to their friend Grace, who lived across the country.

Naomi, Grace, and Sid had been friends since kindergarten, but Grace moved away several months before the girls started high school. Now, they kept in touch over Snapchat. They often sent inside jokes or shared random moments.

TALK ABOUT IT

- **Do you spend time with friends online often? Why or why not?**
- **What are some benefits of staying connected online? What are some drawbacks?**
- **Do you prefer spending time with friends online or in person? Why?**

A few hours later, Naomi looked for a reply from Grace. But Grace hadn't even opened the message yet! "That's weird," Sid said. "Maybe her phone died."

Naomi said, "But she's posted on Facebook today. Why do you think she won't answer our snaps?"

When Naomi clicked through the app, she realized that Grace hadn't looked at *any* of the messages they had sent that week. It made her feel hurt. She'd sent some fun videos of her playing with her dog, who Grace loved. She also wrote several heartfelt messages about missing her friend.

"Maybe she just doesn't want to talk to us anymore," Naomi said sadly. "I mean, she looks like she's busy with new friends now."

"Maybe, but I can't believe she would just ghost us," Sid said. "Did we say something wrong?"

"I don't think so," replied Naomi. She tried to remember whether she'd said anything mean. But now that she was thinking about it, she couldn't even remember the last conversation she'd had with Grace! Naomi had been so busy with the spring musical that she hadn't realized how much time had actually passed.

"Well, if Grace wants to reach us, she knows where to find us," Sid said, and chomped on a carrot loudly. Sid meant to show that she was annoyed, but Naomi couldn't help giggling. Sometimes Sid was a drama queen.

TALK ABOUT IT

- **Do you think ghosting is a fair way to end a relationship? Why or why not?**
- **How can friends who live far away stay in touch? Do you have tips for others who may not know what to do in a similar situation?**

***

For multiple days, the unopened snaps in Sid, Naomi, and Grace's group grew and grew. Instead of saying "Miss you," Sid and Naomi started asking, "Where are you?" Not only did they wonder where Grace was, but they started to feel frustrated their friend hadn't reached out.

Naomi spread her fingers out on her kitchen table and continued painting her nails. Next to her hand, her phone screen lit up. It showed another snap from Sid. Still, no response from Grace. Naomi sighed.

"What's wrong?" Naomi's dad asked. He was also sitting at the table writing important dates in the family calendar.

"Nothing."

"It doesn't sound like nothing," her dad said gently.

"Well, it's just that Grace hasn't responded to our snaps for more than a week," Naomi said. She sighed. "At first, I thought she might be busy. But now I feel like she's ignoring us."

"Have you called her to check in?" Naomi's dad asked.

"No," Naomi said. She screwed the lid onto her nail polish bottle.

"Why not? That seems like an easy way to answer your question."

Naomi rolled her eyes. "We don't really call each other unless it's an emergency. Plus, Grace could call us if she wanted to talk or explain why she's not responding."

"OK, OK," Naomi's dad said. "Well, I'm sure she isn't trying to make you feel bad."

Naomi didn't think Grace was either, but her feelings were still hurt. "I hope not. But maybe she's making new friends and doesn't need us anymore."

"Maybe." Naomi's dad gave a small shrug, but dropped the subject.

***

During lunch a few weeks later, Naomi's phone rang.

"It's Grace!" Naomi said. She felt mixed emotions when she picked up the phone. She was frustrated with Grace, but she was also excited to hear from her.

She was frustrated with Grace, but she was also excited to hear from her.

"Hello?" she said. Sid slid onto the cafeteria bench next to Naomi to listen.

"Naomi! I know it's your lunch hour. Are you free to catch up?" Grace asked.

"Yeah, we haven't heard from you in a long time. Why didn't you answer our snaps?" Naomi asked.

"Oh, gosh, I totally forgot about Snapchat!" Grace said. "I deleted it a few weeks ago and started using a different app. It's really popular with my friends out here. I thought I sent you a snap about it and how I was switching over."

TALK ABOUT IT

- **Have you ever been in a situation where online communication caused a misunderstanding? If yes, what did you do? If not, how can people avoid misunderstandings online?**
- **If you were in Grace's position, how would you have felt about Naomi and Sid? What questions might you have for them when you called on the phone?**

Naomi looked at Sid, who appeared just as confused as Naomi felt. She couldn't remember ever getting a message about a new app. "Yeah, you forgot that part," Naomi said.

"Oh, I'm so sorry!" Grace said. She sounded relieved. "I'll text you about the new app and send you my username and everything after this. Actually, I did think it was odd you hadn't gotten around to trying the new app. I sort of thought you might have just moved on without me."

"We were thinking the same thing," Naomi said. "But I'm glad you called because we miss you!"

People
Search
My Status
My Page
My Friends
My Photos
My Videos
My Groups
Apps
Pages
Interests

Sid nodded, and the lunch period bell rang.

"Oh, we've got to go to class. But send us your new information so we can stay in touch!" Naomi said. She felt relieved that they were all still friends and had new ways to keep in touch. But she reminded herself to not just rely on social media to talk to her friends, especially since not every person has every single app.

Naomi and Sid threw away their garbage and walked to class together.

"I'm so glad we finally heard from Grace," Sid said.

"Me too!" Naomi agreed. "But I do feel kind of silly for not just calling her sooner." Her dad had been right. Calling is an easy way to check in with someone instead of making assumptions over social media.

Calling is an easy way to check in with someone instead of making assumptions over social media.

"Yeah, me too," Sid agreed. Just then, their phones buzzed. Grace had sent them a group text message with the new app and her information. Naomi responded with a heart emoji and texted, "Can't wait to try it after school!"

ASK THE EXPERT

At first, Naomi and Sid were annoyed that Grace stopped responding. They could've called her, but they worried that Grace was moving on with friends she saw in real life at her new school. At the same time, Grace thought Naomi and Sid were moving on without her. However, the girls missed each other and realized how important staying connected online was.

Friends can support each other in tough times through social media. In 2018, 81 percent of teens felt more connected to their friends' feelings because of social media. However, you can't hug a friend over the internet! It's also harder to interpret tone in a message. You may not know whether something a friend wrote is a serious statement or a joke.

The key to staying connected with friends is balancing time together online and offline. Spending time together online can be easy. You can chat at any time of day or whenever you have a free moment. But try to keep a healthy balance of in-person interactions too. One of the best ways to strengthen offline relationships is by using online platforms to communicate and find a time to get together in real life. When people use social media to plan hangouts, they emphasize the importance of being together.

GET HEALTHY

- Call close friends. Talking on the phone can feel more personal because you get to hear your friend's voice. Consider phone calls for important conversations or just to catch up and show you care.
- Be open to saying sorry and accepting an apology. Staying in touch online isn't easy. Girls may forget to respond or type the wrong words.
- Don't immediately think the worst. Miscommunicating online happens often. Instead of jumping to a bad conclusion, ask your friend what they meant first.
- Plan time to get together in real life. Friends who spend time together in person can enjoy sharing life experiences and bond in different ways.

THE LAST WORD FROM EMMA

When my brother and sister went off to college, we were suddenly living in three different states. We had different class schedules and extracurricular activities, which made it hard to keep in touch. The two people I used to see every day were now gone. At first, that made me sad. My whole life and what I was used to had changed, seemingly overnight. I didn't know how I was going to spend my time without my siblings at home.

After a few weeks, we made sure to stay connected through social media. They sent pictures of cool places they visited, and I sent funny videos of our dad falling asleep on the couch. Sometimes social media caused misunderstandings, but ultimately, it helped us stay close until we saw each other next.

CHAPTER THREE

WATCH OUT!

Maybe you completed your Facebook profile with your relationship status, hometown, school, and birthday. Your Instagram biography might list your phone number or Snapchat username. You may list a personal email address on your blog. Bit by bit, each piece of information may not seem like a big deal to have online. But all your personal information can easily get into the wrong hands when you freely post it online.

When girls put their personal information online, they can put themselves at risk. In extreme cases, girls can be followed by stalkers or targeted by sexual predators. They may receive unwanted, inappropriate images or texts. Stalkers may find out where they live. Staying safe online is important. When in doubt, share less information and use privacy settings.

The allure of gaining thousands of followers prompts some people to make their accounts public instead of private. It can be exciting to have people following your content from all over the world. But it also opens you up to some dangers too. M.J. had a private Instagram, but her friend Willow teased her for being too careful. See what happens when M.J. decides to make her account public.

M.J.'S STORY

Smack! M.J. hit a tennis ball with her racket. It landed *way* out of bounds, so much so that M.J. had to laugh when she ran up to the net. "Wow, I think I was aiming for the court on the other side of town," she said.

Her teammate, Willow, laughed as she chased after the ball. She then jogged over to M.J. and placed the ball in M.J.'s hand. "Let's be done for the night," Willow said. "My arm feels like cooked spaghetti!"

The girls sat next to each other on the bench while changing into different shoes and packing up their rackets. M.J. took a moment to catch up on some Instagram notifications she'd missed during their practice session. She hadn't had Instagram for very long and was just getting the hang of the app on her new smartphone. She turned her phone around to show Willow a cute video of her cousin's new puppy.

"Oh, that reminds me," Willow said, lacing her shoes. "I tried following you on Instagram, but it looks like your account is private. I wanted to see if you had any photos of your little sister, since you tell the cutest stories about her!"

"I tried following you on Instagram, but it looks like your account is private."

"Oh, yeah, she's adorable," M.J. agreed. She zipped up her tennis bag. "Sorry I didn't see your follow request last night! I'll accept it right now."

"No worries," Willow said. "You know, you could just make your account public. You wouldn't have to keep track of requests, and I could easily see all your cute family pictures."

"I've thought about making my account public, but I don't know. Is it really that much better?" M.J. asked. She wiped her forehead with the back of her hand. It seemed dangerous that anyone could see her photos. Her current Instagram followers were only people she went to school with or who she knew from playing tennis.

TALK ABOUT IT

- **Do you have public or private social media accounts? Why?**
- **Why might some people prefer to have a private social media account instead of a public one? What about the reverse?**
- **What arguments could M.J. make to Willow for wanting to keep her account private?**

Willow nodded as she scrolled through her phone. She passed it over to M.J. *Whoa*, M.J. thought. Willow had *thousands* of followers! And she posted stuff pretty close to what M.J. did: photos of tennis meets, selfies, cute or funny things she saw around town.

"Oh, absolutely, I love it," Willow said. "I get lots of likes on my photos, and I'm posting because I want people to see them anyway."

"I guess," M.J. said, unsure. She handed the phone back. "But do you ever get messages from random people?"

Willow shrugged. “Sometimes, but it doesn’t bother me,” she said. “In fact, I’ve made a couple friends through those random messages!”

“Really?” M.J. asked. She’d never made an online friend before.

“Absolutely! I post about a lot of concerts I go to, so I get lots of likes from music fans,” Willow said. “Mostly I get to chat with other people about music and stuff. Sometimes I have to delete spam messages, but that happens everywhere.”

“Yeah, I get spam advertisements in emails almost every day,” M.J. agreed. “Well, maybe I’ll try making my account public and see if I like it!”

“And don’t forget to accept my follow request,” Willow said. They laughed as they walked to their cars in the parking lot.

***

After showering and finishing her homework, M.J. opened the Instagram app on her phone. First, as promised, she accepted Willow’s follow request. Almost immediately, Willow went through and liked her most recent posts. M.J. laughed and shook her head as she tabbed over to her settings page. M.J. paused for a moment, her thumb hovering over the screen. Did she really want to make her profile public?

I can always change it back if I don’t like it, M.J. thought as she changed her profile to public. Now people didn’t need to get her permission to see her photos.

Nothing changed immediately. She didn't gain hundreds of followers the second her profile became public. M.J. breathed a sigh of relief. Everything seemed to be the same as it was before. She added a few photos to her story of the popcorn she was making as a late-night snack, then forgot about Instagram and went to sleep.

However, when M.J. checked Instagram the next morning, she saw that she'd gained ten followers! *They must have found me through my story*, she thought. Someone she didn't know reacted to the finished popcorn with a clapping emoji. When M.J. clicked through to their profile, the person had several mutual friends with M.J., all people from the tennis team. M.J. felt good about people liking her posts, but she also felt odd because she didn't really know them.

She sent the profile to Willow in a direct message and asked, "Do you know who this is?"

Willow responded almost immediately. "Oh, that's Micah," she replied. "They're Cathy's sibling." Cathy was another person on the tennis team, though she and M.J. rarely played together. But now that Willow mentioned it, M.J. remembered seeing someone who looked like Micah hanging out with Cathy after their recent meet.

TALK ABOUT IT

- **Have you ever gotten spam messages? Where? How does spam make you feel and why?**
- **Have you ever gotten messages or comments on your social media posts that made you uncomfortable? What did you do about it? What advice would you give to others for how to handle the situation?**

M.J. felt a little better. She still didn't know Micah at all, but at least she knew how Micah got to M.J.'s Instagram account in the first place. She followed Micah back.

***

Over the course of the next week, M.J. gained almost 100 new followers on Instagram. Like Willow had said, many of those were spam accounts that were clearly fake people with lots of random numbers after their usernames. But some of them were real! A few had even reached out to M.J. about funny things she'd put in her Instagram story.

On Friday after tennis practice, M.J. and Willow went to a sandwich shop together. They snapped a picture with their huge meals.

"This looks so good," M.J. said.

"Yeah, my stomach was rumbling for almost all of practice," Willow agreed.

"I'm going to post this picture—are you excited to star in my public Instagram posts now?" M.J. joked.

"I feel honored," Willow joked back.

Within a few days, strangers were commenting on M.J.'s Instagram as if they knew her. She smiled at comments with positive notes or funny emojis. But one comment stood out. Some guy mentioned the sandwich shop that she posted a photo in and said he went there often. M.J. didn't recognize his username, so she kept scrolling. But the fact that he said he went there often stuck in her mind. Something just didn't feel right.

She decided to look at his profile. She noticed he seemed much older than her. She shuddered. His message made her uncomfortable now. She did not want him to know when she went to the sandwich shop or for him to try and meet her there. She blocked him, which made her feel better. But now she worried that other strange

TALK ABOUT IT

- **What are the positive and negative aspects of having a public account? A private one?**
- **What tips would you give to others for how to stay safe online?**

users like him could also be following her since she hadn't been checking people's profiles recently.

I could go through all my followers like I used to and make sure I know how people found me online, she thought. However, going through each person and keeping up with new people would take lots of time. But M.J. knew she needed to do something, so she changed her account back to private. She could go through the accounts over time and delete the ones that made her feel uncomfortable. Maybe some people were OK with public social media profiles, but M.J. didn't like the experience at all.

ASK THE EXPERT

M.J. tried having a public account, but she felt odd getting random likes and comments from people she didn't know. When a man messaged her about the sandwich shop she went to, M.J. felt the situation had gone too far. She decided to make her account private again.

Using privacy settings is one way to protect yourself from strangers. Another way to stay safe online is to not share your passwords. In 2015, one in five teens said they shared a password with a friend. Some gave their password to a friend so the friend could log in, post a picture on the other person's account, and log out. This put people at risk for cyberbullying. It also gave a friend the chance to post something inappropriate.

Other things people should watch out for online include fake profiles, violence, and sexual harassment. People can easily lie about their age, gender, and name. They can even steal photos from another person to use as a fake profile picture. Sexual harassment can happen in different ways. For instance, a stranger may send or ask for nude photos.

You can't control how other people act online. But you can take steps to protect yourself. If you're considering making a public social media profile, talk to your parents or a trusted adult first.

GET HEALTHY

- Be modest with your personal information. Avoid or be careful giving out your birthday, phone number, address, school, work location, and financial information.
- Use privacy settings. If given the option, use privacy settings to keep strangers from viewing your profile without your permission.
- Talk to a trusted adult about uncomfortable interactions online. If you get a message that makes you feel uncomfortable or unsafe, be sure to tell an adult so he or she can help you take further action.
- Don't be afraid to block someone. With most social media, you can block or report any suspicious accounts.

THE LAST WORD FROM EMMA

When I was in high school, my family took a trip to Disney World in Florida. I brought my smartphone so I could share photos on social media. On the first day of vacation, my mom saw me take a picture at the airport. She quickly asked me not to post our location or the dates of our trip. I wondered why. She saw my puzzled look and said that she didn't want people talking about how our house was going to be empty for a whole week. An empty house could seem like an invitation for a burglar or group of teens wanting to pull a prank. I hadn't even thought about that! I just wanted to post fun photos from the trip.

Ever since that trip, I rarely update my location. I still post pictures from vacations or fun outings, but I post them once I get back. Keeping my location private makes me feel better about how I stay safe online.

CHAPTER FOUR

POST VS. REALITY

If you've ever posted online, you've probably felt some posting pressure. You might have edited pictures so the colors look just right. Maybe you asked friends what to write in a caption or text. Perhaps you created and deleted several posts before officially sending something out.

Many teens feel pressure to show a certain type of content in order to get the most likes or comments. This content is often positive or makes them look good to others. While the content may be true, it doesn't show the whole situation. Social media profiles are edited. People can change the way they look or the language they use. They post only selected photos, videos, and text. Even people who post candidly must leave out parts of their life. Social media captures everyday moments, but it is not an accurate reflection of normal life. It can harm teens' idea of reality in different ways.

Girls may be tempted to compare themselves with others they see online. Comparison can create feelings of inadequacy, anger, and envy. Girls motivated by negative emotions may put others down in order to feel better about themselves. Or they may avoid talking about having bad days or admitting their insecurities because they want to seem in control. Additionally, "likes" and comments reward a person's posts. Not getting enough of these rewards can cause stress, depression, and anxiety.

Not getting enough of these rewards can cause stress, depression, and anxiety.

Cho felt self-conscious after seeing a friend's post, but being honest with herself and her friend helped Cho see the difference between the post and reality.

CHO'S STORY

Cho lay on her back in the grass and scrolled though her WeChat moments. It was a nice day outside, and for the first time in months she didn't have a basketball game on the weekend. Time to relax, nap, and use social media outside so she could pretend to be doing something. Her moments were full of photos and

updates from her friends. Most of them documented where people were going on the weekend, typical places like the mall, the movie theater, and the new Mexican restaurant down the street.

One post on WeChat caught her eye. It was a video of her friend Vera on a boat trip with her family. The video panned over a clear blue sky, bright sun, and sparkling water. Next it showed Vera laughing with her family while her dad drove the boat. Vera splashed some water at her brother, who retaliated by taking a bite of her peanut butter sandwich. Cho laughed along while watching. Vera and her brother were always getting up to trouble.

A few minutes later, Vera posted a photo. It was of a school of fish swimming under the boat. The fish were so close that the light reflected off their blue scales. Cho wasn't a huge fan of fish in general, but the photo was really lovely. That led Cho to scroll through some of Vera's other photos. On Friday after school, Vera had gone to a movie with some of her friends from the robotics

club. And Saturday morning Vera had posted a photo of a fancy croissant and coffee drink she'd had before going on the boat trip.

Cho frowned and rolled onto her stomach, the grass poking against her skin. Vera had been out doing a lot of fun things while Cho had been lying in the grass and watching TV on the couch. She wished she'd filled up her weekend with fun plans rather than sitting around doing nothing. She *never* did anything fun like that, especially after her parents got divorced last summer. Between trips to her mom's house and basketball practice, Cho barely had time for anything else.

TALK ABOUT IT

- **How does seeing posts of what other people do make you feel? Does it most often make you feel better or worse about yourself? Why?**
- **After seeing Vera's post, Cho regretted what she did over the weekend. Has social media ever made you think or feel that way?**

Vera's perfect life made Cho sad. She thought about deleting her WeChat entirely. If she didn't have any interesting photos to post, why did she even bother having one in the first place? Instead, Cho went back into her house to watch more TV. At least then she didn't have to look at Vera's fun vacation.

***

On Monday, Cho and Vera went to an ice cream shop after school. They stood in line together and peered through frosty glass at different flavors.

“After we get our ice cream, let’s take a picture with them,” Cho suggested.

“Totally,” Vera agreed. The girls moved closer to the register. “So what did you do this weekend?”

“I was just at my house,” Cho said. She felt like she needed to say something more, so she added, “The weather was really nice, actually. How was your family boat trip?”

“It was amazing!” Vera said. She went on to describe the highlights. She enjoyed the beautiful weather, the fresh seafood her dad grilled, and her brother’s surprise visit. He went to college in another state and worked and lived there now. Vera’s family didn’t see him much anymore.

"He totally surprised us!" Vera exclaimed. "Dad opened the front door and he was standing there with his bag packed, but he told us all week that he wouldn't be able to come. I loved having him there."

"That's awesome!" Cho said. The girls paid for their ice cream and sat at a table to eat it.

"So you and your brother don't fight much anymore?" Cho asked. Before he left for college, Cho remembers Vera complaining about her brother often. She said he hogged the television and ate so much that the refrigerator rarely had food in it.

"Well, not exactly," Vera said. "We did get into a big fight on the boat. I pushed him in as a joke, but he didn't think it was funny. He yelled at me and pushed me in too, but he shoved harder because he was mad and not joking as much." Vera looked down and shrugged. Cho was surprised. Vera's description of her trip and the video she posted online made it seem like the trip was all fun and games.

"Well, not exactly," Vera said. "We did get into a big fight on the boat."

"Oh, I didn't realize you got in a fight again," Cho said.

TALK ABOUT IT

- **Do you ever do something or wear something just because of what you can post about it later on social media? Why or why not?**
- **In your opinion, should people post more "real" or difficult moments instead of just highlights? Why or why not?**
- **Do you think social media can ever completely show the truth about a person's life? Explain your answer.**

"Yeah, bad moments aren't very popular to post about," Vera said. She frowned and ate a big scoop of ice cream.

Cho licked her ice cream cone and thought about what Vera had said. *It seems obvious now, but she's right,* Cho reflected. *I hardly ever see posts about people fighting or having a bad day.* Cho was glad Vera was honest about her relationship with her brother. It reminded Cho that she can't always believe what she sees on social media. She ate a little more ice cream and decided to be honest back about how her weekend really was.

"To be honest, staying home while I saw friends like you making cool posts about your weekends made me feel a little down," Cho admitted.

"You shouldn't feel bad," Vera said. "Honestly, people stay home most weekends. They just only post when they do something different."

"I guess," Cho said. The more she thought about it, the more she realized lots of other people spent their weekend at home. She remembered seeing several friends post images of television screens or movies they were watching. And her neighbor's car was in their driveway all weekend, so they probably stayed home too.

"Plus, you got to relax and enjoy the weather. That sounds like a good weekend to me," Vera said, and smiled. Then she stood up to throw away her dish. When she got back to the table, she said, "Oh, we forgot to take a picture with our ice cream!"

"Plus, you got to relax and enjoy the weather. That sounds like a good weekend to me," Vera said.

Cho dramatically smacked her forehand with the palm of her hand. Vera laughed.

"Let's still take a picture anyway," Cho said. She ate the final piece of her cone. They posed for a picture, with arms around each other's backs, to remember their afternoon together.

ASK THE

EXPERT

Cho felt bad about herself after seeing Vera's social media post. But Vera admitted her post only showed the good parts of her weekend vacation. When Cho and Vera were honest with each other, they realized that social media posts are often not the same as reality.

Often, social media is a highlight reel of someone's life. Not only do people want to show off and remember good times, but they know positive posts are more likely to get likes and comments. Additionally, most teens think that you can show a different side of yourself on social media. In other words, social media is a place people can act differently or hide parts of their true self.

This gap between what others post on social media and what reality is like can create mental health risks for teens. Some research links depression to social media use. These studies found that the amount of time spent online matters less than how many social media sites a girl uses. Teens who use three or more different sites are at higher risk of depression or related negative symptoms. Once you realize the difference between social media posts and reality, you can set out to protect your mental health. Life isn't just about the highlights. Everyone has good days and bad days, even if they don't post about them.

GET **HEALTHY**

- Don't worry about making the perfect post. Focus on enjoying life off-screen.
- Try posting about real life instead of just highlights. When you are honest online, your posts could encourage others to show their life in a more realistic way.
- Stop scrolling. If you are feeling down after looking at social media, then take a break. Focus on what good things have happened in your day so far or how you can end the day on a good note.
- Make a list of activities you enjoy and do them. Having fun in real life reminds people that social media is just one way to connect with others.

THE LAST WORD FROM **EMMA**

When I started using social media as a teen, I struggled to know what to post. I had friends who updated their location and profile daily. But that seemed like a lot of work to me. Also, I didn't want to reveal too much information on social media. Once a post is made, it's online for many people to see.

After seeing a variety of other people's accounts, I decided what would be best for me. I treated my social media as a memory bank. I posted lots of pictures from holidays, birthday parties, and celebrations such as winning a competition. I also used it to capture spontaneous moments such as a pretty sunset. Most important, I remembered that everyone uses social media for different reasons. Instead of comparing another person's post with my life, I focused on enjoying each day whether I posted about it or not.

CHAPTER FIVE

TRYING TO KEEP UP

Have you ever felt like keeping up with social media is impossible? By the time you check more than one app, you could have new posts and messages waiting for you in the original one. Pictures from family and friends fill Instagram. Twitter feeds update constantly. Snapchat stories replay moments you missed.

Keeping up with friends, news, and your favorite celebrities is fun. Being online can give you opportunities to learn and explore. You can join a fan page of a band, see news stories from around the world, and watch videos to gain knowledge or skills. Even in busy times, you may feel like keeping up with social media is worth it.

However, the constant flow of information can be exhausting. There are a lot of things happening in your town, in your state, and around the world. It can be challenging to know what to focus on and which sources to trust. You may also feel responsible for keeping track of *everyone's* activities, and feel guilty if you miss someone's latest post.

Mackenzie experienced stress from trying to keep up, and so did her friend Bea, though they were stressed for different reasons.

MACKENZIE'S STORY

Zzzzt. Zzzzt. Mackenzie felt her phone buzz in her pocket. She waited until class was over to check it. In the hallway, she pulled out her phone, and the screen lit up. Notifications from several apps gave her a hint of what she had missed online during class. Her mom had texted her asking what she wanted for dinner. Facebook showed which of her friends had birthdays. Snapchat linked her to a live video from her favorite reality TV show. Twitter updated Mackenzie about a news story she'd been following recently. She looked at all the updates and then selected the news story. Now that she was old enough to vote, she wanted to be informed about the candidates.

Notifications from several apps gave her a hint of what she had missed online during class.

Mackenzie read the article as she walked to her locker.

She glanced up often to make sure she didn't run into anyone. But suddenly, her phone was pushed to her chest as she collided with someone.

"Sorry!" both girls said at the same time. Then Mackenzie immediately began to laugh. She had run into her best friend, Bea.

"Are you OK?" Bea asked. She was laughing too.

"Yeah, just reading about the upcoming election," Mackenzie said. "One of the candidates said something wild, so it's blowing up on Twitter. You?"

"I was checking Facebook. Did you see Autumn invited us to a party this weekend?" Bea asked. She glanced down at her phone again.

"No, I haven't seen that yet. I'll check it later." Mackenzie looked at the time on her phone. "I've got to stop at my locker before class," she said. "See you in seventh period!"

"Yeah, see you!" Bea replied.

***

Mackenzie didn't have a chance to finish reading the article about the election until after school. While heading to the bus, she chatted with Bea and checked all of the notifications that had piled up during the day. It was their afternoon ritual: they'd sit together and scroll, occasionally showing each other what had happened on their phones. Then they'd go to Mackenzie's house to work on homework until Bea's mom got off work at the hospital.

TALK ABOUT IT

- **How do you keep up with information online? Which apps or social media do you use most?**
- **Do you keep a smartphone with you at all times? Why or why not?**
- **Do you check social media frequently during the day, or do you set aside larger chunks of time to check them? What could be the benefits and consequences of your habits?**

Mackenzie felt like no matter how many news articles she read, there were always more. She tried to remember which candidates had which policies, but sometimes she struggled to keep the facts straight. Additionally, it didn't help that some reporters and news organizations were biased. Some journalists didn't report all of the information to make one candidate seem better than another. Others didn't report truths at all, but only posted conspiracy theories. Sometimes Mackenzie became overwhelmed reading about the upcoming election. Every time she refreshed Twitter, there would be another handful of articles or posts to read. She had so many tabs open that she could barely remember which articles she'd already read.

Mackenzie felt like no matter how many news articles she read, there were always more.

After boarding the bus, Mackenzie put her phone facedown on her lap and sighed. She'd hoped that chatting with Bea would help her mind stop spinning, or at least distract her from the big decision she would eventually have to make about voting.

"Who are you going to vote for?" Mackenzie asked Bea.

"I have no idea," Bea said. "I've been meaning to look up information about the candidates, but I always end up checking other apps first. Then by the time I find out what's happening with friends, I'm behind again." She waved a hand in disbelief. "There's just so much information."

TALK ABOUT IT

- **Where do you get news? How do you separate facts from opinions? Do you have any tips for other people who might be navigating this same space?**
- **Have you ever felt pressure to keep your social media updated or to know what your friends are doing each day? What do you do when keeping up gets stressful?**

"I know what you mean," Mackenzie agreed.

"And I feel so much pressure to always be online," Bea continued. "If I don't like someone's post right away, I feel like they think I don't care. And that time when I missed Autumn's message on Instagram, she thought I was purposefully ignoring her and got really upset. I had to drive to her house and apologize."

"If I don't like someone's post right away, I feel like they think I don't care."

"Yeah, I remember that," Mackenzie said. Eventually Autumn and Bea had made up, but it was an awkward time for their group of friends.

Zzzt. Zzzt. Mackenzie's phone buzzed. Her mom wanted to know when she would be home for dinner. She typed a reply, and Bea unlocked her phone. When Mackenzie looked up, Bea was getting ready to take a selfie.

"Smile!" Bea said, and she put her face close to Mackenzie's so she would also be in the picture. The girls grinned, and Bea snapped the shot. She posted it to Instagram, and Mackenzie liked it right away.

***

Before school the next day, Mackenzie popped into the US Government teacher's classroom. She thought Mr. Murphy could help answer a few of her questions about some candidates' policies. She knocked on the classroom door before walking in. The room was empty. Mr. Murphy sat at his desk grading papers.

"Hi, Mackenzie," he said, smiling. "How have you been? I haven't seen you since you were in my class last year."

"Yeah, that was one of my favorite classes," Mackenzie replied. "I miss being in your class this year because I'm sure you're talking about the upcoming election. That's actually why I stopped by. I was hoping you could help explain some of the candidates' policies. I've been reading news articles online, but I still feel a little confused." She sat down at the desk across from Mr. Murphy's and rested her backpack on her lap.

"Oh, OK, well, which candidates and policies are you talking about?"

"Well, all of them, I guess," Mackenzie began. "I follow several candidates on Twitter as well as the major news networks.

It seems like every time I finish an article, there's four more recently added. It's so hard to keep up! Sometimes I get distracted and have to start an article over. But then I realize I've been ignoring my friends to read the news."

TALK ABOUT IT

- **What are some benefits to using social media for news and social updates?**
- **What are some drawbacks to keeping up online?**
- **How can girls stay up-to-date in a healthy way?**

"You seem really busy," Mr. Murphy said.

"Yeah, I have a million things to do and not enough time to do them," Mackenzie agreed.

"Well, based on what you just told me about feeling like you can't keep up with the news or your friends and family, I'd guess that social media is making you more stressed."

"Yeah, maybe it is. But I still have to try to keep up with the election, right?"

"I'm sure you could still keep up with family and friends by talking with them instead of checking posts online. Why don't you try taking a break from the digital world? After all, the news will still be available in a week." He smiled.

Mackenzie liked the sound of that. It would be nice to feel like she didn't have to be glued to her phone. She'd even gotten in trouble a couple times for checking Twitter during class.

"And while you're on a digital break, write down a few questions about the candidates' policies, and we can chat again later," Mr. Murphy said, bringing their conversation back to the starting point. Mackenzie smiled. She grabbed her backpack and stood up.

"Yeah, that sounds like a good idea. Thanks for the advice," she said, walking toward the door.

"No problem, Mackenzie. See you later."

Mackenzie left the room and turned her phone on silent. She put it in her pocket and already felt relieved without the pressure of keeping up on her mind.

ASK THE EXPERT

When Mackenzie felt overwhelmed by news articles, she turned to talk with Bea. Bea was stressed about letting friends down on social media, so she constantly checked her accounts. Despite the pressure to stay informed, the girls still found time to laugh with each other while hanging out. Additionally, Mackenzie realized taking a break was one way to deal with stress.

You may feel guilty if you don't respond immediately. These unspoken rules of the social world, such as responding to popular hashtags or keeping a Snapchat streak going, can all lead to anxiety about social media. And studies have found that your anxiety increases when you have multiple social media accounts and a large circle of friends to keep up with.

During adolescence, many teens begin using social media or use it more than they did as children. But being online more can lead to stress. The brain is flooded with information. It works hard to understand, process, sort, and remember everything. The constant activity can be tiring in many ways. People who "unplug" protect themselves from getting worn out from keeping up. Unplugging is about focusing on activities that are not online. It gives the brain time to rest and lets someone recover emotionally and mentally so they can enjoy being online later.

GET HEALTHY

- Set aside time for being online and time to unplug. Balancing time on social media and time off it is a way to stay up-to-date and stay healthy.
- Be aware of how much time you spend online. Journal about your media use and feelings to see how it might affect you emotionally, physically, or mentally.
- Talk with friends in person when drama happens online. Meeting face-to-face shows a person's true intentions, and it can help solve fights or misunderstandings among friends.
- Trim your list of friends and followers. You don't have to be responsible for knowing everything about everyone. By sorting through your followers, you can reduce the number of posts you see and time you spend trying to keep up.

THE LAST WORD FROM EMMA

In high school, I felt pressure to keep up with my friends' posts. At one point, my friend group had an unspoken contest to see who would notice someone's post first. If you were first, you would often comment, "First like!" with an emoji. Being first to like or comment on a post also showed you were close to the friend who posted, so it was a way to prove your friendship or popularity too. While it was fun to have multiple friends notice my posts right away, it was also stressful to feel like I had to be constantly checking social media.

After a few months, we realized friendship wasn't just about keeping up online. Hanging out without social media was still fun regardless of social media posts.

CHAPTER SIX

STOP CYBERBULLYING

It's easy to joke and be sarcastic with friends online. A friend may intentionally post an embarrassing photo of you where you're making a weird face. You may find that friend's Facebook profile still logged in on your laptop and post a joking status pretending to be them. These jokes are often harmless—or at least, they may start out that way. A joke can easily be turned into something hurtful online. People may misunderstand a rumor and spread false information. Someone could copy a photo and draw on it or change the point of a joke.

The lack of physical connection between people online makes it easier to insult someone. You can't see a person's face or reaction if you're not in person or over video. This physical distance can lead to accidental insults or purposeful cyberbullying. Cyberbullying is attacking, targeting, or otherwise hurting someone by means of a digital device. It includes mean texts, false rumors, embarrassing photos, and hacking someone's account.

People often feel safer behind a screen, and they may joke or post about certain topics that they normally wouldn't in person. Unfortunately, Letícia learned that cyberbullying can be painful.

LETÍCIA'S STORY

"I want to get six inches off," Letícia told the hair stylist firmly. She had been flip-flopping all day on whether she actually wanted to go through with the drastic hairstyle she'd been dreaming about all summer. But she knew that it was just hair: it would grow back eventually. She didn't want to chicken out at the last minute. "Please," she added, realizing she had maybe come on a little *too* strong.

"OK, going for a bit of a change," the stylist said, smiling at Letícia in the mirror. "I think it's going to look great."

"Thanks," Letícia said. She took a deep breath when the stylist pulled out the scissors and exhaled when the first large chunk of hair fell to the ground. No backing out now!

The stylist cut and styled her hair, then blow-dried it and applied some product. She showed Letícia how to care for her new hair length. When Letícia stood up, she felt so much lighter with all of that hair missing. And when she put her glasses back on and could really see her new hair in the mirror, she watched herself grin. It was the perfect back-to-school look.

Before driving home, Letícia took a few selfies outside the salon. The sun was shining, her hair smelled like the special salon

hairspray, and she felt great. She posted two selfies on Facebook to show her friends the before and after look of her haircut.

Right away, people liked and loved her post. Her grandma commented with approval too. She said, “Beautiful! Call me soon to chat, love, Grandma.” Letícia smiled reading it. *I should call her later,* she thought.

***

The next morning, Letícia woke up earlier than she normally would for school. Not only did she have first day nerves but she wanted to make sure she could style her hair like the stylist had. With only a few minutes to spare, Letícia rushed out the door and headed to school.

Letícia’s friend Courtney squealed over her haircut in the parking lot before school.

“I love it!” Courtney said. She touched the edges.

“Really?” Letícia asked. “This morning it felt weird with so much hair gone, but I’m still getting used to it.” The girls stopped at Letícia’s locker before going to Courtney’s. Letícia unzipped her bag and pulled some folders out to replace them with textbooks.

“Yeah, I think you totally rock a short haircut, and your post last night was so cute,” Courtney added. Then they stopped at Courtney’s locker so she could swap out her books too.

“Oh, thanks! Of course, my grandma commented right away,” Letícia joked. “Here, look what she said.” Letícia held out her

phone so Courtney could see the post. "I think she used about eight heart emojis."

As soon as Letícia found her post on the Facebook app, she saw a new comment. It was from another girl at school, Shelby. Letícia and Shelby weren't close, but they saw each other in class often and lived a few streets apart. Mainly, Letícia knew Shelby because she dated one of Letícia's ex-boyfriends.

Shelby commented, "Who wore it better?" with a picture of a celebrity on the red carpet with a similar haircut. Suddenly, Letícia felt self-conscious. Her smile faded. She thought that if anyone actually compared the photos, her casual selfie would look worse. Letícia looked at more comments below, and it seemed that Shelby's group of friends all chimed in. They said things like "Definitely not Letícia!" and "omg, what a no brainer," with laughing emojis.

"Seriously!? Look at this." Letícia showed her phone to Courtney. Courtney's mouth dropped open, and tears welled up in Letícia's eyes. To make matters worse, Shelby and her friends were huddled together at the end of the hall. Letícia looked down fast. She didn't want any of them to see her and make fun of her hair in person.

"Geez, it's like Shelby asked them all to comment mean things. Are you OK?" Courtney looked at Letícia.

TALK ABOUT IT

- **How can you know whether a rude comment is an accident or not? If your feelings get hurt, does it matter? Why or why not?**
- **Have you ever received unkind comments on a social media post? Would you try to ignore them or do something else? Why?**

"Yeah," Letícia took a deep breath. Her feelings were hurt, but more than that, she blamed Shelby for all the mean comments. She also felt mad.

"Do you want to talk to Shelby about it?" Courtney asked. "Her locker is just down there." She pointed to the end of the hallway. "And it looks like the other girls are going off to class now." They watched as Shelby's friends walked around the corner and were gone.

"Will you come with?" Letícia asked.

"Yeah, of course," Courtney said.

"Hey, Shelby," Letícia started. "I just saw your comment on my Facebook post from yesterday. Why did you post that comparison? And did you ask all of your friends to comment too?"

"Relax," Shelby said, rolling her eyes. "It was just a joke."

TALK ABOUT IT

- **Have you ever posted or said something harsher online than you normally would in person? Why do you think you felt comfortable acting differently online?**
- **Would you have confronted a bully like Letícia did? Why or why not?**
- **How is Courtney being a good friend to Letícia?**

"It wasn't funny," Letícia replied as Courtney shook her head. "It really hurt my feelings."

"We used laughing emojis," Shelby said, "so you could see it was a joke."

"That made it look like you were laughing *at* me!" Letícia said. "Your words still hurt, and all your friends joined in, which made it worse."

Shelby frowned. "Hey, I'm sorry. I guess I didn't think about it before I commented. I can delete my comment if you'd like."

Letícia nodded and tried her best to smile. "I'd appreciate that," she said. Letícia was proud that she had stood up for herself and talked to Shelby about her feelings. Even though the comments were on social media, they still made her feel upset in the real world.

"Your words still hurt, and all your friends joined in, which made it worse."

TALK ABOUT IT

- **What would you do if one of your friends was being cyberbullied? How could you help your friend?**
- **Do you think Shelby's comments weren't cyberbullying because she didn't intend them to be? Why or why not?**

ASK THE

EXPERT

Letícia was feeling good about her new haircut until she saw mean comments on her post from a girl at school. She decided to confront Shelby with her friend Courtney and received an apology. The apology didn't take back the hurtful words, but it showed that Shelby took responsibility for her actions.

If cyberbullying happens to you, you can first try ignoring it or asking the person to stop. But cyberbullying isn't always resolved quickly. You can also reach out to a teacher or trusted adult. Those people can help get the police involved if necessary or if the attacks continue.

In 2018, 45 percent of teens felt overwhelmed by drama online, and 52 percent reported seeing cyberbullying of themselves or others. Even though the problem starts online, it can cause real-life consequences. Girls who keep quiet about mean texts or messages they get can be more strongly affected by cyberbullying over time. No matter how cyberbullying starts, you can take steps to end it and the negative ways it has affected your life.

GET HEALTHY

- Before posting, ask yourself whether you would say the same thing in person. Many hurtful posts happen because people aren't face-to-face to see the other person's reaction.
- Stand up for yourself. Confronting a bully could reveal that the insult was a mistake or lead to an apology.
- Watch for signs of cyberbullying in close friends. Reach out to friends and trusted adults to help stop the attacks.
- Block or unfollow people who are mean online. Take advantage of selective features in social media to protect yourself and have only positive followers.

THE LAST WORD FROM EMMA

One of my close friends was cyberbullied in high school. She hid the mean comments for a few weeks but eventually broke down and admitted she was being hurt. She wanted to block the bully on social media, but worried that would cause the bully to be meaner in person. Together, we told the school principal, who called the bully's mom. The bully was forced to apologize, and she admitted she was going through a tough time when she sent all the mean messages. She also knew that didn't make her actions OK, but she hoped my friend could forgive her.

Social media and hiding behind a screen makes it easier for people to send hurtful messages. But girls can support each other in tough times by listening and reaching out for help.

CHAPTER SEVEN

THINK BEFORE YOU POST

Posting on social media is just a few finger taps away. In seconds you can create, edit, publish, and control memories of your life. Not only is fast-paced technology cool and fun, but it is a key way people communicate in today's world.

However, instantly making a record online may come back to hurt you later. Adolescence is a time of learning and growth, and everyone makes mistakes. But mistakes captured in immature or thoughtless posts can be nearly impossible to take back. Mistakes may be as harmless as misspelling a word, but they could also be posts that spread hurtful or untrue ideas. Angry words, mean photos, and threats—even if someone doesn't mean them—can lead to serious consequences. Sometimes those types of posts are classified as crimes. The sender can face repercussions at school or with local government.

Girls who take their time posting show they care about others. They can think about who is included or left out of a post. They can think about who will see it and what type of message the post sends. After all, positive posts can be used to brighten people's day.

> Girls who take their time posting show they care about others.

Sylvia learned the importance of thinking before posting one weekend when she shared too much information about her friend Esther.

SYLVIA'S STORY

The sun went down in the local park. Sylvia sat on a plaid blanket next to her friend Esther. Eventually, the large white screen in front of them lit up.

"It's starting!" Esther whispered excitedly. This was the first time they had been to a movie in the park.

"I'm glad we decided to stop studying and come see the movie," Sylvia whispered. "We can review the questions again tomorrow, and then we'll be ready for the test on Monday."

"Totally," Esther agreed. "And what my mom doesn't know won't hurt her. Hey, let's open the popcorn now," she whispered back. Esther hadn't told her mom about the movie in the park. She'd just said they would study together for their math test on Monday.

"Good idea," Sylvia said as she pulled open the bag of popcorn they had brought, and the girls munched on it during the first few minutes of the show. Suddenly a small dog ran between the girls' arms. Sylvia gasped and pulled the bag of popcorn away.

"Sorry!" The dog's owner whispered loudly, from a few blankets away. She yanked on the dog's leash. "C'mon, boy, that's not our popcorn," she said, and pulled him back to her blanket.

Sylvia and Esther looked at each other and giggled. "Maybe we could just give him a handful?" Esther suggested.

"Yeah, I'll ask," Sylvia said. Quietly, Sylvia talked to the owner and then gave her a handful of popcorn to feed her dog throughout the movie.

I've got to write a story about this for a blog later, Sylvia thought. She had originally begun a blog for her creative writing, but over time the content expanded to include photos and stories about things happening in her own life. The story of this cute dog startling her and Esther would be a great addition.

***

The next day, Sylvia crafted a story about her night at the park for her blog. She posted it and got several comments right

TALK ABOUT IT

- **Sylvia partly uses her blog as a way to remember fun times with friends. Do you like to keep track of some memories online? Why or why not?**
- **In your opinion, is some information too personal to be shared online? Why or why not?**

The story of this cute dog startling her and Esther would be a great addition.

away about how funny her story was. Sylvia smiled. She didn't think anything of her post until she got a call from Esther.

"Sylvia! Why did you have to write about that night?" Esther sounded distressed. "I didn't tell my mom we were going out that night, remember? She thought we spent the whole afternoon studying and then just stayed in and went to bed."

"Oh, I'm so sorry," Sylvia said. "I totally forgot. Should I take it down now?"

"Sylvia! Why did you have to write about that night?"

"No, it's too late. My mom's already seen it," Esther said. She sounded glum.

"What's wrong?" Sylvia asked.

"Well, I have to miss Dee's Halloween party this weekend."

"No!" Sylvia said. "We were supposed to go together. I can't do a partner costume alone!"

"I know, I know," Esther said. "But I don't think my mom's going to change her mind."

"Maybe I can apologize to her too," Sylvia suggested. "I'm sorry. I just thought it was a good story. I didn't think about how it might affect you."

"It's OK. I know you didn't mean it," Esther said. "Well, I've got to go. My mom's calling me now. She gave me extra chores for lying to her too. See you later."

"Bye," Sylvia said. She regretted her blog post for multiple reasons. She felt bad that she had caused her friend trouble, and she knew the party would not be as much fun without Esther. Next time, Sylvia would remember to think about who was in her stories and their possible consequences before sharing on her blog.

"I just thought it was a good story. I didn't think about how it might affect you."

TALK ABOUT IT

- **Have you ever posted something you regret online? If yes, what did you do about it? If not, what would you do if that happened?**
- **Is there a way Sylvia could have still told the story on her blog without getting Esther in trouble? How?**
- **What do you think about before you post online? Do you have any tips or suggested questions people should ask themselves before posting?**

ASK THE EXPERT

Sylvia thought she was just sharing a fun story on her blog. She didn't think about who might see it, such as Esther's mom, or that she couldn't take it back. She learned the importance of thinking before you post when she accidentally got her friend in trouble.

If you're posting about something controversial or emotional, taking a few minutes to think can help you calm down and see whether you want to change your post or not post it at all. Thoughtful posts can lead to good experiences. People can express themselves in creative ways. They can practice communication skills and explore new ideas.

Everything you post online becomes part of your digital footprint. A digital footprint is a collection of all your online activity. It includes your profiles, the comments you make, the accounts you follow, and the information you share or like. A person's digital footprint grows as they do more online, and it is difficult to erase. Past messages, tweets, photos, and more can be traced. Additionally, future employers and schools often check social media before hiring someone or accepting an application. They want to see what kinds of overall messages someone's posts send. For that reason and more, girls should think before they post. Being thoughtful keeps you, your friends, your family, and your future's best interests in mind.

GET HEALTHY

- Think before you post! Ask yourself whether the post is appropriate. Would you be proud to show it to others or take responsibility for it in the future?
- Consider who may see your posts. People can interpret messages and photos in different ways, so being thoughtful could help avoid hurting someone's feelings or causing trouble.
- Give yourself extra time. If emotions are high, or you're posting about a tricky topic, don't rush to post. Waiting an hour or a day gives you time to calm down and see whether the post sends the right message.
- When in doubt, don't post. Posts are nearly impossible to take back, and negative ones could hurt your reputation.

THE LAST WORD FROM EMMA

I treated my Facebook and Instagram like photo albums during high school. I posted about special memories and events so I could easily look back on them. I had multiple friend groups, and to avoid hurting people's feelings, I made an effort to think about who was in photos I posted and who wasn't in them. I didn't want people to feel left out or like I didn't value their friendship.

On the other hand, some people I knew treated their Facebook as a diary. Sometimes their opinions were harsh. While I learned a lot about those friends from their posts, I know they regretted sharing so much. By the end of high school, one of my friends deleted her old profile and created a new one. She wanted to separate herself from old posts as much as possible even though she knew the posts would never completely disappear.

CHAPTER EIGHT

HOW MUCH IS TOO MUCH?

You've probably had days when you felt like you wasted your time online. Maybe you scrolled endlessly through Facebook or watched video after video on TikTok. Somehow, time flew by and you didn't know how it got to be so late. On the other hand, you've also probably had days when you didn't touch your phone for hours. How can one girl experience both types of days?

Well, online technology can be a part of most daily activities, from making food to tracking sleep, so girls have to decide for themselves what's the right amount of screen time. It's normal to have days when you are less active than others. But if a girl isn't aware of how much she is on social media, it could easily eat up her time.

Many teens don't realize how social media can control their brains. A brain scan study proved that the reward region of the brain is activated by "likes" on social media. In other words, when you get a like, your brain associates using social media with rewarding, positive emotions. This region of the brain is extra sensitive during adolescence. For that reason, teens may crave more time on social media or feel negative emotions when they don't "get enough."

When Nevaeh was forced to spend a week without her phone, she realized how much social media had interrupted other parts of her life.

NEVAEH'S STORY

"No!" Nevaeh shouted, as her phone fell into the sink of dirty dishes. She reached in, and after a few seconds, she located her phone and pulled it out. It was sudsy and dripping. She hastily dried it off on a towel and tried to turn it on. The screen was blank.

"C'mon," Nevaeh said as she stomped her foot. Now was *not* the time for her phone to break. She hadn't even caught up on her Snapchat streaks for the day! She got out a plastic container and filled it with rice. Then she set her phone in the rice and hoped

the tiny grains would soak up the water in her phone. After she finished the dishes, she told her parents about the accident.

"I'm hoping my phone turns on in the morning, but I don't think the rice trick will work. So I'll probably need to get a new phone," Nevaeh said.

"That's a bummer, sweetie," one of her dads said. "I'll look into getting you a new phone, but it may not come for a week or two."

"OK, thanks," Nevaeh said. She was lucky her dads could get her a new phone at all, but two weeks felt like forever. She went to bed frustrated with her bad luck.

***

The next day was Saturday, and as soon as Nevaeh woke up, she reached for her phone. She felt the smooth top of her nightstand before she remembered her phone was sitting in a pile of rice.

"Ugh," Nevaeh moaned, and rolled out of bed. As she predicted, her phone still wouldn't turn on. She told her dads and asked to borrow one of their phones to call a friend. She logged into her Facebook account from her dad's phone and searched for Lucille's profile. Lucille had her phone number listed in her About Me section. Nevaeh clicked on the number to call Lucille.

TALK ABOUT IT

- **Have you ever been without a connection to social media for more than a day? How did you feel about that situation?**
- **Nevaeh feared missing out on activities with her friends. Have you ever felt that way? What did you do about it?**

"Hey, Lucille!" Nevaeh said.

"Hey, Nevaeh!" Lucille answered. "Why are you calling from a different number?"

"Well, my phone is currently sitting in rice because it fell into water yesterday," Nevaeh said.

"Oh, no, that's why you didn't answer my text last night," Lucille said. Nevaeh instantly worried that she had missed something important.

"What did it say?"

"Well, I texted you last night to see if you wanted to go apple picking, but you didn't answer, and we've already left," Lucille replied. Nevaeh felt a mix of emotions. She was frustrated with her bad luck and upset she was missing a fun activity with friends.

"That's fine," Nevaeh said, trying not to cry. "Just call me as soon as you're back. Well, call my dad's number, and let me know if there's any other plans. I feel so out of the loop!"

Nevaeh felt a mix of emotions. She was frustrated with her bad luck and upset she was missing a fun activity with friends.

"I will!" Lucille said. "Oh, gotta go! Bye!"

Nevaeh went back to her room. She couldn't distract herself on social media or even look up somewhere fun to go until Lucille was back. Her family only had one computer, and one of her dads was using it for work right now. She looked around her room. She saw some books, but she had too much energy to read at that moment. *I wish I could text my friends' group chat right now,* she thought. Then she saw her diary stacked under some books. She decided to vent by journaling. She felt better after a few minutes. Then she made a list of things to do to keep her mind off the fact that she wouldn't have a phone for several days.

She started by listing things to do around the house; *I should probably clean my room*, but she definitely didn't *want* to do those activities. Then her list grew to include plays, trips, and movies she wanted to see. She actually got excited thinking about these activities! She remembered the school's play was coming up, *Fiddler on the Roof*. Several of her friends were in it, and it would

be lots of fun to go. Additionally, spring break wasn't too far away, so Nevaeh wrote down some places she would be interested in visiting. Then she went downstairs to ask her dads about planning a vacation.

Nevaeh wrote down some places she would be interested in visiting. Then she went downstairs to ask her dads about planning a vacation.

However, one of her dads had gone out for a run, and the other was still working. Nevaeh decided not to bother him. She thought about going on TikTok and tapped her sweatshirt pocket before remembering again that her phone wasn't there. Her frustration picked up again. She wondered when Lucille would call. She looked outside.

The weather is nice enough for a hike, she thought. *That's a good way to keep my mind off the fact that I'm missing out on apple picking, and it'll keep me busy.* Suddenly, she was lacing up her tennis shoes and opening the door.

"Dad, I'm going out for a walk. I don't have my phone, but I'll be back by four o'clock."

"OK, have fun!"

Nevaeh went on a hike, and the afternoon passed quickly. After dinner, Lucille called her over for a bonfire, and Nevaeh was glad to be included in her plans.

***

Nevaeh's list came in handy over the next week. She was able to use the family laptop a few times to check social media, but over time Nevaeh worried about getting online less and less. Lucille called her to let her know about plans for going to a movie one night and going to a party another night. So Nevaeh didn't worry about missing out. She always finished her homework and often went outside in the afternoons or journaled about more spring break plans. Her dads had approved a vacation! She got more sleep than usual because she wasn't up late watching YouTube videos or scrolling

TALK ABOUT IT

- **Would you willingly give up your phone for a week? Why or why not?**
- **How can girls set healthy limits for spending time online? Do you have any tips to share?**

She felt better than she had a few weeks ago when she was tired and stressed about always having homework to do.

through her Twitter feed. She felt better than she had a few weeks ago when she was tired and stressed about always having homework to do.

"Nevaeh, your phone is here!" one of her dads yelled from the front door.

"Thanks. Can you put it on the counter?" Nevaeh said. "I'm going out for a hike with Lucille, and I'll set it up when I get back."

"You don't want to do it right away?" he asked. He looked surprised.

"No, I don't need it when I'm with a friend." She smiled and turned to leave.

ASK THE EXPERT

Nevaeh's first reaction to losing her phone was panic and frustration. But being without her phone gave Nevaeh a chance to do other things she enjoyed. She found a way to still meet up with friends, and by the time she got her phone back, she had a fresh perspective on how to set healthy limits for tech in her life.

If it's hard for you to imagine life without social media, you're not alone. More than 40 percent of people thought social media would be hard to give up. One reason screen time is difficult to self-regulate is because it affects your brain. Social media can affect your sleep, too, and sleep impacts you emotionally, mentally, and physically. A British study found that 20 percent of teens wake up in the middle of the night nearly every night to log on to social media. A lack of sleep can affect a girl's mood by making her more stressed. It can make her mind unfocused or heighten existing mental health problems. It can affect her body by making her immune system weaker.

The key to using social media is mindfulness. Be aware of how much time you spend online and how it makes you feel. Girls who prioritize a device may find themselves wishing for a deep connection with a human. Girls who focus on the people in their lives are likely to figure out a healthy balance for using social media.

GET HEALTHY

- Journal about your favorite activities and put your list in a visible spot. Seeing fun things to do can help stop you from spending too much time online.
- Set boundaries for yourself and others. Choose times or places where you will be device-free. They could be your bed, the dinner table, or special events.
- Turn toward a person instead of a device. Making eye contact with someone or putting a device away during a conversation shows you care about the person you're talking to.
- Don't be too hard on yourself. Learning how to balance social media in your life may not happen overnight. You may slip up or go through a big life event and have to change your ways again and again.

THE LAST WORD FROM EMMA

One of my classes in high school was about social media and technology. In it, my teacher asked us to imagine a perfect day. We wrote down what we would do the minute we woke up to the minute we went to bed. I wrote about how I wanted to spend time with friends and family, go to church, take a hike, and eat breakfast food for dinner.

After we spent time journaling, my teacher asked how many people imagined that they would check social media the moment they woke up. No one raised their hand. Next, she asked how many people reached for their phone as soon as they opened their eyes on a typical day. Many hands rose in the air. She encouraged us to think about how technology helped or hindered us from living our best lives.

A SECOND LOOK

Throughout this book, we have followed a girl who met someone online and then in person for the first time, another who stayed in touch with a friend far away, a girl who dealt with cyberbullying, and a girl who discovered that unplugging from social media has some benefits.

Some of these stories may have been relatable. At times, they may have made you a little uncomfortable. If you felt stressed at times while reading this book, you may ask yourself what was making you feel that way. Perhaps it has something to do with how you use social media, or the fact that when it comes to being online, we don't always have a clear picture of what is normal versus abnormal, or good versus bad.

For example, most kids know posts are different than reality. But making a decision such as "How much is too much?" may not be so straightforward. So, relying on your own instincts and on what feels right for you becomes very important. But even a girl who stays absolutely true to herself may find herself in a difficult position, such as being targeted by a stranger online. It is important for girls to develop a balance of time on- and off-screen, while still allowing themselves the space to enjoy social media in safe and responsible ways.

Even if you feel embarrassed by a past post or hurt by a miscommunication with a friend, you are experiencing very common and normal emotions. Remember, don't beat yourself up for thinking or even doing something unique or new. Learn from your choices, and pay close attention to your own reactions. The idea is to create healthy social media habits that will help you express yourself in a way that feels right for you.

XOXO,
EMMA

PAY IT FORWARD

A healthful life is about balance. Now that you're aware of some risks and benefits of social media, pay it forward. You know what to focus on, so practice and share your knowledge with a friend too. Remember the Get Healthy tips throughout this book, and take these steps to get healthy and get going.

1. Be careful when you meet someone for the first time in person. Meet in a public place, and tell parents or other friends about your plans in case you need them.

2. Staying in touch online isn't easy. Try not to jump to bad conclusions. A confusing message may just be a miscommunication. Be ready to apologize if you make a mistake or ask a friend to explain what they really meant.

3. Use privacy settings for your accounts and protect your personal information by keeping it secret. Avoid posting or giving out your birthday, phone number, address, school, or work location to someone you recently met online.

4. Think before you post! Ask yourself whether the post is appropriate or whether it could hurt someone's feelings.

5. **Keeping up with news, events, and updates on social media can be exhausting. Don't be afraid to unplug for a few minutes, hours, days, or even weeks at a time. Use a journal or schedule to find a healthy balance of time with and without your tech devices.**

6. **Remember that social posts are not the same as reality. Take a break from social media if you feel down after looking at it. Create a list of activities you enjoy so you can focus on enjoying life off-screen.**

7. **Everything linked to your account is part of your digital footprint. Future employers and schools may look at your posts to see whether you have a positive or negative reputation.**

8. **Watch for signs of cyberbullying in close friends, such as a change in behavior or avoiding school. Confront the bully or reach out to trusted adults to help stop the attacks.**

9. **Ask a parent or trusted adult to share an example of a post he or she made, or one a close friend made, and later regretted. See what you can learn from his or her story.**

GLOSSARY

biased
Displaying prejudice in favor of or against one thing, person, or group compared with another, usually in a way considered to be unfair.

candidly
Honestly.

catfish
Someone who creates a false identity online in order to trick someone else, oftentimes to lure someone into a relationship.

controversial
Inciting debate over a matter of opinion.

ghost
To suddenly cut off contact with someone and not give an explanation.

meme
An image or video that appears all over the internet and has a certain, often funny, meaning.

predator

Someone who targets a person in order to gain something, often aggressively and without concern for the person's feelings or safety.

spam

Unwanted messages and texts; electronic junk mail.

stalker

A person who follows someone obsessively.

traced

Connected or followed back to someone or something.

vent

To talk or communicate, usually with intensity, about a bad experience in order to express feelings and understand what happened.

ADDITIONAL

RESOURCES

SELECTED BIBLIOGRAPHY

Anderson, Monica and Jingjing Jiang. "Teens' Social Media Habits and Experiences." *Pew Research Center*, 28 Nov. 2018, pewresearch.org. Accessed 28 Feb. 2020.

"Social Media: The Difference between In-Person and Online Communication." *WJHG*, 15 Jul. 2016, wjhg.com. Accessed 28 Feb. 2020.

FURTHER READINGS

Harris, Duchess, and Nancy Redd. *Growing Up a Girl*. Abdo, 2018.

McKee, Jonathan R. *The Teen's Guide to Social Media . . . & Mobile Devices: 21 Tips to Wise Posting in an Insecure World*. Shiloh Run Press, 2017.

Perdew, Laura. *Online Identity*. Abdo, 2017.

ONLINE RESOURCES

To learn more about using social media responsibly, please visit **abdobooklinks.com** or scan this QR code. These links are routinely monitored and updated to provide the most current information available.

MORE INFORMATION

For more information on this subject, contact or visit the following organizations:

Common Sense Media

650 Townsend St., Suite 435
San Francisco, CA 94103
commonsensemedia.org

This organization aims to help people learn about technology and health. It is a resource for parents and teachers to find out about healthy and unhealthy technology and habits so they can help young people use technology wisely.

Girlshealth.gov

200 Independence Ave. SW, Room 712E
Washington, DC 20201
girlshealth.gov

This website is part of the US Department of Health and Human Services. It aims to give young girls information about health, relationships, bullying, and their future.

US Department of Health and Human Services (HHS)

200 Independence Ave. SW
Washington, DC 20201
hhs.gov/web/social-media/index.html

The HHS department educates people about ways to stay healthy. It has information about how to be safe online.

INDEX

ABOUT THE AUTHOR

EMMA HUDDLESTON

Emma Huddleston lives in Minnesota with her husband. She enjoys reading, writing, and swing dancing. She has three sisters and three brothers, and she is an aunt! She hopes this book reminds girls of the importance of living life off-screen and helps them create healthy habits as they grow up.